all
i ever wanted

all
i ever wanted

relationships, marriage, family

Read, laugh, learn and Conquer!

(Carol) Daniel

Carol A. Daniel

Mission Possible Press, USA
Extraordinary Living Series

The Mission is Possible.
Sharing love and wisdom for the young and "the young at heart," expanding minds, restoring kindness through good thoughts, feelings, and attitudes is our intent. May
you thrive and be good in all you are and all you do...
Be Cause U.R. Absolute Good!

All I Ever Wanted, Relationships, Marriage, Family
Copyright © 2013 Carol A. Daniel.

Published by Mission Possible Press
A Division of Absolute Good
P.O. Box 8039, St. Louis, MO 63156
orders@absolutegood.com

Book design by Maureen Cutajar
www.gopublished.com

ISBN 978-0-9852760-4-1

Dedication

To my husband, Patrick, who told me
I needed to write.

To my mother, Rosella Keeler, who told me
I needed to fly.

To my sons, PJ and Marcus, who told me
I needed to give them a sister.

Sorry about that.

Acknowledgements

There are so many people who have had a hand in making my life what it is today. I'm so thankful to God for who He is and for being true to His word.

I have to thank my husband, Patrick, who told me years ago that I needed to write. He has stood by me while my work took me away, and he never complained (about that). I once questioned whether I deserved such a fine man, and now I believe that I do! Love you, my King!

To my greatest joys, next to their father, Patrick Daniel, Jr. and Marcus Isiah Daniel, my sons. I once feared that I couldn't have children, so seeing you grow each day into young men truly fills my heart. I still sneak into your rooms and watch you while you sleep. I know, I know, but I love you so!

My parents, Isiah and Rosella Keeler, have always been examples of perseverance and hard work. You loved me even when I wasn't so lovable, and for that, I thank you. And Mom (Sweet Potato Head), thanks for always praying for me!

My siblings, Billie, Douglas, Al and Nicole, will always be a part of me no matter where I go or what I do. I am so fortunate that each of them married spouses who have become friends, Vanessa, Yvette, Stephanie and Glenn.

To the best mother-in-law a girl could ask for, Catherine Daniel. You raised a fine son. Thank you for that. I am nothing without the love and encouragement of my family and friends. Michelle "Whassup" Black! You know me through and through, and that makes life all right. Knowing you are a phone call away has always made the tough times easier to take.

HM's: Sherry, SherryMac, Lois and Nash. My praying, crazy, creative friends, I can't imagine my life without you. To my Bishop and First Lady, Dr. G. Vincent Dudley Sr. and Glenda Dudley, you changed my life! To my KMOX family, you're just the best and funniest newsroom EVER! And to my *Great Day St. Louis family*, thank you for welcoming me into the world of television. Publisher/friend Jo Lena, the task master, or should I say midwife?! Patrick and I know that seeing you at The Best Steak House that night was meant to be.

Contents

Letter From Little Carol Keeler

———— ✤ ————

This is a hard letter for a nine-year-old to write. I have so much I want to tell you and so much I want to know.

Will I be happy? Will I be tall? I really want to be tall. That way I can be a model. No, I don't feel really pretty now, but maybe my face will change and I'll be pretty one day. Do you feel pretty now? I hope so.

What will it be like when I am a mom? Will I stay home and not work like my mom? I think I want to be a businesswoman. I would like a big family. Will I have girls or boys or both? I hope to have a girl first and a boy second. That way, she won't have a big brother who throws pillows at her or pushes her too high on the swing, and she falls and breaks her arm!

What is it like to be married? What will my name be? Mommy and Daddy are apart a lot because he's a soldier. I miss him, and I think she does too. Remember how much fun you had with Mommy while Daddy was away? You went to the grocery store together.

You were her only girl for a long time. You even slept in the same bed in that trailer when Daddy was in Vietnam, do you remember? Mommy said you were a wild sleeper, and she'd wake up with your feet in her back! She thought you were so funny!

I remember once when we all piled in the car and drove Daddy to the airport. He was wearing his uniform, and I knew he was leaving. Daddy rubbed his whiskers on my face.

I always loved that. Then, I saw him kiss Mommy! My tummy did flip-flops. When I get married, will my husband kiss me like that when he goes away to work? What will it feel like? Mommy seems sad, but she's not really saying much. Will I be sad when my husband goes to work?

I hope you remember how much you loved going to school. You didn't always feel like the smartest, especially in algebra. You were such a funny, friendly girl. But you loved your teachers, especially the one who taught you how to knit, and the one who taught you how to sew. Those blue jeans were the best! Did you ever make a sweater?

Carol, Mommy says, "You shouldn't smile at everyone. You're too friendly." I don't really understand what she means. But I hope we stay that way.

Love,
Me

Growing Up Keeler

My Parents in the 80's
Rosella and Isiah Keeler

I envy the people who can remember every detail of their childhood because I am not one of those people.

I am the fourth of five children born to Isiah and Rosella Keeler. I have three older brothers—Billie, Douglas, and Al, and one younger sister, Nicole. Billie was born in Fort Hood, Texas. Douglas and Al were born in Nuremberg, Germany, while my sister and I were born in Fort Leonard Wood, Missouri. I bring that up because my sister and I often reflect on the fact that they got to travel early in our father's military career, but after I was born, Fort Leonard Wood was home. I did go to Germany once as a toddler but I don't remember one bit of it! People always want to know how many different places I've lived in. When I tell them two, they cock their heads to one side with a look of confusion on their faces. Yeah, I know! Military brat and no stories of enrolling in five schools in four years! No such luck for me.

What my siblings and I do have in common is that we all went to the same high school.

By the time I got there, Coach Hayes, the popular boys' track and basketball coach, simply called me by my last name, Keeler. I don't know if he even knew my first name, but that was okay with me. I thought it was cool. I was impressed that he knew me at all.

I was on the drill team in the sixth grade. There must have been 50 of us in our homemade wrap-around black skirts and black long sleeve leotard tops. That was one of my first public performances, and I couldn't get enough of the pom-poms! I decided to try out for cheerleading in the seventh grade. I just thought with my booming voice, I was destined to cheer my team on to another touchdown or another basket. I tried out every year and made the squad for six straight years through high school. We were a close knit group, and wearing my uniform on Fridays in school was a source of pride.

Cheerleading wasn't the gymnastics sport it is today.

I also played volleyball one season as a freshman, and honestly, it scared me to death. I'm only 5'4," and I have no vertical jump. I could serve well enough, but I never liked being on the net because those girls would spike that ball with such ferociousness that I would stand there thinking, *If this ball hits me, I'm gonna get knocked out!* I didn't last in that sport.

Track was my other outlet, in part, because of the coach, Coach Becky Oakes. She was so encouraging. I wasn't even one of her top track stars, but she treated us all the same and yelled at us all the same when it seemed we weren't taking practice seriously or weren't giving our all at track meets. I'll never forget the season she put me on the triple jump. Now remember, I have no vertical jump, and I discovered I also have no horizontal jump. Coach Oakes told me track meets are all about points, and every point counts. So my goal was to do well enough to earn a few points and to try and jump far enough to land inside the pit. I also discovered that inside the pit is where the sand was. If you didn't jump far enough, you'd hit harder ground. Often, I hit that harder ground. But I earned a point or two. Thankfully, someone else took over the triple jump that could actually jump!

I'll be honest. I loved high school, but of course there was drama! I had boyfriend drama, which turned into mommy drama! I promise I'll explain shortly. But growing up in Fort Leonard Wood was so much fun. We walked for miles. We stayed outside until the streets lights came on. We went on picnics, went bowling, sledding, played tennis, built tree forts in the woods, picked strawberries and went swimming (or should I say, I took swimming lessons over and over again). It seems I was never inside for long.

I do remember my mother often forcing my older brothers to take me with them, something they did not really want to do. One sunny day, we walked from our house to the horse stables on base. There was an old oil barrel that had been strung up between some trees that you could straddle and ride like a swing. I got on, and my brother, Douglas, began to push. I told him he was pushing me too high, but he didn't stop. I fell off, onto the ground, onto my left arm, breaking my wrist. I'm not sure why my brothers didn't try to get any help at the stables; instead, we walked at least a mile, all the way back home. Douglas had his arm around me, and he kept telling me it was going to be okay and not to cry. I'm also not sure if he was comforting me because I was hurt and crying or because he knew he would get in trouble. I don't remember his punishment at all. I only remember when the emergency room doctor pressed on my wrist, I kicked him in the face, knocking off his glasses.

I had that cast in school and because it was my writing hand, I thought I'd get a break from the teacher. NOPE! She didn't slow down for me at all. Did I say I was seven years old? To make it even more frustrating, my little sister had just been born, and as much as I wanted to hold her, I really couldn't for a couple of weeks.

Drill Sergeant's Daughter

―――――∽∿∽―――――

Broken arms and track meets aside, growing up in Fort Leonard Wood for me was all about having a Drill Sergeant for a father. Unlike kids whose parents worked in an office, a store or even a school, I never got to go see what my father did for a living. I only learned from movies that I saw as an adult. Even back then, I knew the control, respect and fear his position received.

One of the places I used to love to go was the bowling alley. They had the best French fries ever! Once, a trainee approached me and began to flirt. It was a weekend, and he had his uniform on. I knew his career in the Army had just begun, and he was likely to still be in basic training. I imagined that he was 18 or 19. I was only 13 or so, and I knew he was too old for me. I was so shocked that this grown man was hitting on me like that, and all I could think to say was, "My father is a drill sergeant, and I don't think you should be talking to me." I've never seen young men scatter like he and his friends scattered away from me. It gave me such a sense of empowerment in who my father was. That became an even greater part of my identity.

I never thought of how hard my father's job was, I just didn't know enough. But I did love the uniform, especially his "Smokey the Bear" hat. He would lay that uniform out each night. My favorite part was when he polished his boots. He opened the round tin of black wax, and the aroma filled the room. He had a white cloth diaper, and he would wrap it around his forefinger and his middle finger, rub it into the wax and then rub the polish into his boots. Then my favorite part came. He would take a lighter and hold one boot in one hand and the lighter in another, and he would heat up the wax on the boots! Nothing would get on the hard wood floors because he spread out newspaper. After heating the wax on the boots briefly, he would polish them again with that cloth diaper.

It may sound odd, but it was mesmerizing to me, from the flickering flame, to the smell of the wax, to the rhythm he always used to polish his boots until they shined. He took such care. Because I never saw him leave in the morning, and there were times when he worked a 24-hour shift, I just loved those nights watching him get ready.

People ask me all the time whether my father was a drill sergeant at home. He really wasn't. My mother was actually the disciplinarian! All those years my father was deployed to Vietnam and Germany, my mom had to take over. I'm not sure whether she became the disciplinarian out of necessity or because it was in her DNA, but she was good at it! I can't count the number of times I was put on restriction for coming home late or talking back, but there was no reasoning with her. I once thought that surely my lie that my watch had stopped would get me off the hook, but no such luck—ever! Not one excuse ever worked with her. She was a stern one. On occasion I would write her long letters explaining my innocence and how she really didn't understand me! She said she understood me all right. I was just disobedient and hardheaded.

I do remember one aspect of what I thought was my father's job that seemed to come home with him. He used to curse a lot. It lasted until my mother taped a *Dear Abby* column to the refrigerator from a woman who wrote that her husband was too profane. The woman wanted to know how to stop her husband from cursing so much. Abby responded by telling the woman that people who curse display a lack of control of the English language. Apparently, that was all it took because I remember my father going cold turkey on the profanity. That was when I learned how much influence my mother really had without saying a word!

The Keeler Men
Douglas, Billie, Isiah and Al

My Mother's Love

———— ⌇ ————

I can see my mother's influence in my life today. I try to clean as I am cooking, something she begged me to do as a teenager. I even put water in pans to soak them and make the cleanup easier, another habit she prayed I would pick up. But for years there was one area where her influence didn't work - the boyfriend department. To hear her tell it, I was the one she worried about the most.

The fact that I did well academically in high school didn't change the fact that my dating life was a mess. To put it mildly, my mother did not like my boy-friend. That began the strained mother-daughter relationship that would last through my 20s. The boyfriend didn't last but the drama stuck around for a while, as did her concern for my well-being.

After high school, I followed in my brothers' footsteps yet again and went to the University of Missouri-Columbia. I was shocked by how unprepared I felt. I quickly began to question the 3.6 GPA I brought to the campus. The college math class with 200 other students felt like Greek. I dropped the statistics class so quickly, I left skid marks in the hallway. I began to feel, "I never should have come to college in the first place." To make my very existence even more questionable, after missing rent, my roommates, I believe, conspired with the landlord to violate my rights and change the locks on our apartment! No notice of eviction, just me on one side of the door and my stuff on the other. Of course, pride entered in and I didn't tell my parents. Instead, I moved in with my then-boyfriend. The icing on the awful cake was the discovery that he had a drinking problem and I had a GPA that barely had a pulse. I decided to try to salvage my college career and transfer. I took my shame and my sense of failure with me to Lincoln University in Jefferson City, Missouri. It was a kind staff member in admissions, who remembered my name during my second visit, who convinced me I needed to be there. It was also the feeling that I had nowhere else to go.

My mother told me that I would have to live alone (really) and she would pay for my apartment. DEAL! Then she said, "This is your last chance." I lived off campus and got to know few people. I was so lonely that first year. I didn't even go to the homecoming parade but I could see and hear it from my apartment window as it went past. I didn't have a car and my father would bring me groceries every two weeks. But soon my mother stopped him and told me, "You need to get your own husband. This one is mine." I did finally make friends and grades. I may still have the letter from the university president informing me that I'd made the Dean's List! I began to feel less like a complete failure.

When I graduated from Lincoln University, I moved

to Kansas City, Missouri. I loved that city! I loved the outdoor concerts, the jazz clubs, the shops and my very own one bedroom apartment with a balcony shaded by dozens of trees. I barbequed on the deck even when it snowed, I had dinner parties for one and I bought a waterbed and a dining room set that officially meant I was a grownup! I worked two and three jobs at a time. I sold cable door to door. I worked retail clothing sales, had a morning news shift on a radio station, was a recruiter for the Census Bureau, and I sold radio and print advertising. When I was about 26, I again thought I was in love.

He started making some radical changes in his life after joining a mosque. His charming demeanor that won me over, quickly soured the deeper he got into the Nation of Islam. He became anti-establishment, which in his mind meant not working for "The Man." It didn't mean that for me, but our relationship quickly became dysfunctional and emotionally abusive. He didn't want me to work although he wasn't working either. No money meant no ability to pay rent and again, I lost an apartment and this time, a great job.

How could I let this happen? I had already struggled my way out of college. I hadn't planned to struggle again. But here I was asking myself, *How does a woman smart enough to get a degree end up in a situation like this?* Pride again entered in and I didn't tell my mother what was happening. I moved in with a friend's parents and for a month, I wondered what I would do and where I could go. I didn't call my mother but she was calling my disconnected line and wondering what happened to her daughter. I finally mustered the courage to call her. I explained some of the story and she simply said, "Come home."

A few days later, my father drove the four or five hours to get me. He loaded my few remaining items into his truck and I moved home to Waynesville, Missouri, where I'd grown up, right outside the base. I hadn't imagined going back to my parent's home. Yet, my life was too precious and I had to reclaim it. I learned *what I never wanted* and what I wouldn't stand for.

My goal now was to get back into my career and regain my sense of self. What I hadn't counted on was my mother and I repairing our relationship. I found a job at KJPW, a country and western radio station making $9,000 a year. That was where I read the obituaries at noon each day, covered the Gulf War and its impact on families at nearby Fort Leonard Wood, and it is where my mother and I had lunch together nearly every day for 18 months.

One day she came to me and said, "I love having you here but you know there's nothing for you here. I think you need to move on." I was stunned. Was she tired of me? I had begun to think of myself as a small town girl settling into a decent life and I was all right with that. But my mom told me, "No, you need to fly."

I knew how hard it was for her to send me back into a world that I had stumbled through. I worried her so much. She worried that I wouldn't graduate from college. She worried that I wouldn't find the right man and get married and have a family. She worried that because of my mistakes, I might not get on firm financial footing. I promised myself I would never worry her again. She tells me now that she was praying for me every night. I'm so happy she's around to see my life today and know that her prayers were answered.

About Relationships

———— ✺ ————

Relationships are necessary, but they aren't easy. You know why? Because people are involved and people have problems and issues in all shapes and sizes. Your father may have taught you how to fish, but it was more challenging teaching you how to love, especially if he never showed you in his relationship with your mother. Parents of a certain generation didn't talk about communication or shared responsibilities or anything, really. They only knew that being a husband meant being a provider. No hugs or mushy words. Mothers cooked and cleaned and had dinner ready when pops got home.

Now books, CDs, articles, talk shows and co-workers surround us with all the answers as to why you can't find that special someone. But we're still hard pressed to really communicate with each other. You've probably heard it before, it's time to focus on becoming the real you.

You may not even know who that is; well now's the time to answer some questions. What do you like? Where do you stand? What makes you happy? What makes you excited? What annoys you? Are you a night owl? Do you like to eat out or stay home? Do you like long drives, the beach, sunsets, dogs or scary movies? Do you love dessert or bacon? Do you talk a lot or are you quiet as a church mouse? Are you a runner or a couch potato? Do you like your legs, your eyes or your hands? Are you afraid of change? Are you selfish? Do you need compliments? Do you hate compliments? Do you avoid confrontation? Do you give until it hurts? Do you have road rage?

It's just a start but knowing yourself first will make it a lot easier to find someone who fits.

And if your heart is broken or you are still upset with your circumstances or have convinced yourself that things will never change, please make a promise to yourself that eventually you will heal and it will get better. Believe that you actually deserve to heal, that you deserve better.

How It All Started

———— ∿ ————

I still reflect on those times when I didn't think I deserved better. I don't want to forget the promise I made to not worry my mother, even though I am the mother of two teenage boys now. My husband and I are now a half a century old and I have notched 17 years at KMOX, one of the most respected radio stations in St. Louis. It seems like yesterday that I got that call from then program director Tom Langmyer.

He was traveling to Memphis on vacation with his family, scanning radio stations on the way. I was sitting in the newsroom of KZIM in Cape Girardeau, Missouri getting ready to go on the air. The phone rings and I hear him say, "You don't know me but I'm Tom with KMOX and we've got a job opening here and I was just wondering if you'd like to apply."

Because others were in the room, I could only answer with, "Yes, of course. Sure. Okay. Got it. Thank you. Bye." Two weeks later I was in St. Louis working at one of the greatest news talk stations in the country.

My husband and I were just about to celebrate our first anniversary in St. Louis when I found out I was pregnant. It was one of those picture-perfect nine months. No morning sickness, no health problems, plenty of energy, and for once in my life, long finger-nails. Once the time came for the baby to enter the world, hours of uneventful labor followed before my husband noticed that each time I had a contraction, the baby's heart rate went down. We told the nurse and before we knew it, what seemed like two dozen people converged on our room, whispering among themselves but telling us nothing. I finally demand-ed that someone explain the grim looks on their faces. We were told that the umbilical cord was around the baby's neck; a very common occurrence and that everything would be fine. My mother, fa-ther and sister were there to see Patrick Jr. come kicking and screaming into the world. I called my sister days later to ask her to "steal" the instamatic pictures my father had taken of me after PJ's birth. Let's just say they were not very complimentary. I should have burned them, they look so bad, but they might come in handy one day when I need to con-vince my son how difficult his birth was.

The memories of being pregnant with my youngest son and his birth are quite different. After two miscar-riages, I was more worried with the news that I was going to have another child. I told very few people at work until after the first trimester with my second child Marcus. I had also taken on a new and longer work schedule just weeks before we got the news I was pregnant. The split shift left me exhausted each and every day for nine months. I also found myself in the worst roller coaster of emotions. Everything set me off and everything made me cry. But we persevered.

One cold day in December, on the way to an interview at Annie Malone Children's Home for a series on Black History in St. Louis, I had a contraction in the car. Later, a doctor's appointment revealed I was already dilated. The next night was the annual KMOX Holiday Radio Show. It's safe to say I was in labor on stage. Just over 24 hours later, I was in full labor but being the stubborn woman that I am, I chose to stay home as long as possible. That was nearly an embarrassing decision. My contractions were now minutes apart and we were crawling across the Poplar Street Bridge from Illinois over to Barnes Jewish Hospital in St. Louis, a 30-minute drive. At the hospital my only question was whether I could still get the epidermal shot. The nurse fooled me into thinking there was actually a chance. Well, there wasn't because I was too close to birth. Less than an hour later, my baby Marcus came into the world. It's called natural childbirth and the only chemical I had in my system was adrenaline.

Everyone told me how quickly the boys would grow and how fast it would go. And they were right; suddenly I'm 50. I realize that my babies are now young men and soon they will be gone. I guess I can't get older and they stay younger. Oh, if it were possible, though!

Career First, Babies Later

It's crazy to think now, but my plan was to be married at 25 and have my children at 26 and 28 because I'd read somewhere that children are smartest when born to mothers who are in their late 20s! I didn't wait on purpose. I just didn't find the right man until I was 30! Millions of words have been spoken, posted, cried and whispered about the issue of women purposely delaying childbirth for a career and then finding that conception later in life is an expensive, perhaps impossible journey.

Where to begin?

I knew I wanted a family of my own when I was nine years old. *That's all I ever wanted.* I always envisioned myself as a wife and mother. As I got a little older, I also saw a fabulous leather briefcase and an equally fabulous career. That was my vision. But it would take nearly a decade for God to lead me to Patrick. I should say that it took nearly a decade for me to give it up and let God do what I apparently hadn't a clue about.

I'll never forget my 30th birthday. I was a very single talk show host for a radio station in Cape Girardeau. I worked 12-hour days, often ending up studying topics at the local library until employees closed up shop and turned off the lights. I worked so long and hard that I wasn't getting to know anybody. A woman I'd met through a news story told me about a nice young man that she thought I should meet. She never told me about his regal cheekbones or his wonderful laugh, just that he had a good job. I began to wonder if he had a third eye and toxic breath!

Our first meeting was spoiled when influenza came to stay in my house for a few days. The second meeting was at a New Year's Eve party. He rolls his eyes when I tell people that I thought he was jailbait when we first met. It turns out that I'm just a few months older than he is. We were married a year and a half later on a day that the rain fell but stopped just in time for the sunshine and me to walk down the aisle together.

I know there are women like their male counterparts, who make the internal decision to focus on their career path and delay family. But there are many women like me, who wanted love and career at the same time but didn't find it. When my husband and I met, we asked each other the same question and were shocked by the answer. Do you have any children? "No."

There is nothing wrong with waiting, but ladies let me tell you the truth about conception, childbirth, career and picky eaters.

Our Wedding Day
Mr. and Mrs. Patrick Daniel

First of all, men make new sperm every three months. But baby girls are born with all the eggs they will ever have, and those eggs get old, sticky and they don't last forever. And friends who have gone through fertility treatments talk about thousands of dollars, painful surgeries and years of disappointment that may or may not end up in joy.

The perception of the biological clock is a reality. A woman's eggs are on a timer. You may want love in your life, but now you are in line for a promotion which means more travel, more client dinners and more breakfast meetings, so who really has time? Right?

Do we have any regrets? Yes. You see, we are 50 and we have two active boys, 13 and 16 years old, while one of my brothers, just two years older than me, is an empty nester! As I try to write this, one child is asking me to buy him a camcorder for a class project while the other wants to make sure I have paid his registration fee for a 5K race in Indiana. What we lacked in financial stability and maturity then, we made up for in energy. How many times have we put the priority on career and 401ks only to realize that energy is as important a commodity? And yes, I know I need to exercise and I need more sleep, but now I'm facing peri-menopause, so who can sleep!

Women have been told, "You've come a long way baby," and we have. However, we still aren't paid like our male counterparts. We still have the glass ceiling, and we still do most of the work at home. And, to add insult to injury, we are hit in the face with the brutal fact that as women, we can be welders or even firefighters and police officers, but the womb won't wait forever. I am here to tell you that you really don't want it any other way. Children need something that no six-figure, demanding career can give them and that's your energy.

And let's face it, six-figure, demanding careers have a way of sapping all the energy that you have, leaving precious little time to pull your angels off the ceiling fan (again).

Balancing Family and Career

My mother's prayers have been answered. I have the wonderful husband, the handsome children and even the awesome career. But I feel like the Vegas act where someone spins a bunch of plates at the same time. That's been my story since the job with KMOX came calling, a few months before Patrick and I celebrated our first anniversary and found out we were pregnant at nearly the same time.

When PJ was born, we lived in downtown St. Louis in a high-rise. But we moved to the suburbs before he turned one.

Other than being a picky eater, he was a happy go-lucky talkative boy who once talked in the car for an entire thirty-minute drive to the airport. He loved nothing more than trains and books about trains. Then pregnant again, four years later, I was gripped by fear. What if my pregnant womb was housing a little sister?!

All I could think about was my rocky teen years with my mother. She once told me that I was the reason she had gray hair.

And now I was pregnant with what could be the ultimate payback, a daughter just like me. I was too tired working that split shift to think about what it

The Legendary Jack Buck
Patrick, Jack, Baby PJ and Me

meant that, with PJ, I craved grape juice, but with this child, I was craving steak!

My husband was worried as well. But I knew his fatherly concerns had to do with his potential baby girl growing up and coming home one day and telling us she was with child. I quickly informed him that I didn't find it much more comforting that our son might come home and say that he had gotten someone pregnant. Besides, I tried to convince him, "Daughters are usually the ones who take care of you when you get old." That made him think.

But again, no baby girl was delivered on December 17, 1999, it was a beautiful chocolate baby boy with dark curly hair and an insatiable appetite. You see, I decided to breastfeed Marcus like I had done for our first child, PJ. At that initial nursing in the hospital, I was a little skittish because it took our oldest two long painful weeks to latch on. But that would not be Marcus' story. He latched on right away and then nursed so long that a nurse walked by my room and doubled back and asked me, "Is he still going?"

I laughed because I was just so relieved. When PJ was born, I had every intention of nursing but no one told me that there could be such pain, such sharp, incredible pain from little gums gnawing on my nipples! I was about to give up but then at 2 am with tears streaming down my face, he finally latched on! Unfortunately, my milk dried up after only three months, but I was able to nurse Marcus for six months. Marcus nursed so long, and my milk was so plentiful, that he seemed more like a drunken sailor with the clear mother's milk running down his cheeks while he tried to get more. He's still greedy to this day.

Together, Patrick and I are dealing with two completely different children. PJ is the quiet, studious one. And Marcus is the outgoing, fearless one. PJ prefers solitary pursuits like the computer he built and game design. One day I woke up and PJ stopped talking and I realized, "Oh my God, he's a quiet teenager." He is his father's child. Marcus would prefer a salad for breakfast and a game of basketball or hitting golf balls into the pond. And he turned out to still be the ultimate payback, a son, just like me.

The Boys and Me
Newborn Marcus and Big Brother PJ

Best Friends

———————◦\◦———————

The one thing both of my sons have in common is their love of Chicago. They've gotten to go because that's where "MELO" lives. My best friend Michelle's place has been one of our main vacation destinations for ten years now. She sold nearly everything she owned, including her car, and moved to Chicago to fulfill a lifelong dream.

The dream was a nightmare for years while she tried to get her personal, career and financial footing. After years of working for various campaigns and elected officials, she was ready for something different. It was different all right. After unemployment sank in, she decided to apply for a job as an airport screener. She thought surely her Master's Degree and her decade in public service would help. She went to an airport job fair and filled out the application at a computer kiosk. Before she could pull out her hand sanitizer, the computer screen lit up with the words, "You are not qualified. We will keep your application, blah, blah, blah!" She told me she thought she was losing her mind. In case you're wondering, the job qualifications for an airport screener at the time were a GED or high school diploma.

She never quit trying though. She decided to work as a temp until something, anything, came along. During one of our marathon four-hour conversations that stretched into the early morning hours, she told me of being hired to work the races in Joliet, Illinois. She said she thought hawking newspapers and making a couple hundred dollars in no time would be easy. Of course not. It was 110 degrees and her female partner was a recovering cocaine addict who couldn't stop talking or moving. The third party who drove them there decided to stay and gamble, once what Michelle described as "slave labor" ended, thus stranding them.

With her sunburn in tow, she finally caught a train back to Chi Town, with the recovering addict along side.

It was midnight and everyone at my house was asleep, so I was muffling my laughter and tears.

During the ride she had determined that the recovering addict wasn't recovering at all, that she was still in fact using. That may explain why during the train ride, the woman, who was white, used the "N" word to describe someone she was upset with. Michelle, exhausted, sweaty, smelly, sun burnt and still essentially unemployed, told the woman to cease-and-desist with such language. Could it get any worse or any stranger? Of course. Michelle, for some reason, had given the woman her phone number, which the woman used at midnight to call Michelle and tell her that a black friend of hers said it's okay to use the "N" word so what was Michelle's problem?

Michelle finally launched her own event planning company and is juggling clients. Both of us know those highs and lows. The lows have shaped us and we are so glad that we've had each other to get through them. She was there when I had my sons and she was there for me when two of my babies didn't make it. She was there when I met Patrick, when I thought we wouldn't make it as boyfriend and girlfriend, and when we exchanged our vows.

I've never stopped telling her that she can do anything and she'd better because the world needs her success. Michelle talked me through my eviction and she was there for me when we bought our dream home. Now we are beginning the journey and the conversation about caring for our aging parents and staring at our own retirement plans in the not-so-distant future.

I heard a woman on a radio program talking about the pressure some wives put on their husbands to listen to everything they say, expecting them react to it, and be interested in it all. I thought, *Why not?* But then the guest said, "That's what your girl-friends are for." I can totally agree with that. Blessed with thirty years of friendship, Michelle and I aren't just friends, we're sisters.

When I turned 50, Patrick gave me a surprise birth-day party. Michelle was one of the surprises, flying in to share my special day. Patrick says he could not have pulled off the party without my girlfriends, the "HM's." Someone began calling us, "Hot Mommas." We aren't sure what she meant but the name stuck. Sherry, SherryMac, Lois, Nash, Cynthia, and me. We try to get together on a regular basis to laugh, eat and pray. Did I say laugh?!?

My sons call us, "The Mommas," which I adore. "Are the Mommas coming?" "Are the Mommas going to be there?" We are all married mothers and that is enough to get a conversation going! We always have something to share, work through or laugh about. Michelle told me, "I'm glad you have them there. I can tell they love you and you love them." I told my sons once, "You don't need a lot of friends, just a few good ones." The HM's and Michelle are living proof.

Best Friends
Michelle and Me

My Husband Is Right!

I don't get to talk to Michelle for hours on end, like I did when the boys were little, but she has followed my transformation from a shopper to a saver. I've had plenty of training to get me there courtesy of Patrick. In 2001 we, like thousands of Americans, got a rebate check from President Bush. What did you do with yours? I'll bet you can't answer. The only reason I can is because of my husband. He decided to immediately deposit it into our savings account.

I will never forget the time that Patrick told me that I was spending our sons' inheritance. That stopped me in my tracks. I had been buying little things for the boys every day. A pack of gum, a balloon, a bag of chips, but I realized that I was setting them up to believe that, with me, came stuff. I never even thought of the purchases as totaling a lot of money. But now I understand that I was fueling in them an unhealthy subconscious concept of finances. That revelation helped me to look at my relationship with money differently and I began to make changes.

Back to 2001 when my first thought was to spend...

On the way to the bank, Patrick asked me to endorse the check so that he could deposit it into our anemic savings account. Of course I signed it. Who doesn't want a cushion, a rainy-day fund? But then I asked why he hadn't asked me what I thought we should do with the check. I know that was a chuckle I heard before he answered me. "I assumed you wanted to put it in the savings account instead of spending it on shoes and expensive dinners."

How was I supposed to respond to that? Of course I wanted shoes, but now I couldn't say so. To do so would support the attitude behind that all-knowing look on his face. Don't ask me how many pairs of shoes I have.

A financial advisor once told us to save three times our monthly salary in a savings account, in case of job loss or a leaky roof. I know it sounds like the impossible dream, especially when a new catalogue arrives with an ivory cowl neck sweater, suede skirt and croc-print boots on the cover model. See how it works? The mind wanders and so does that money.

Now back to the rebate check. I know President Bush's hope was that Americans would spend the money (on shoes and expensive dinners) and help stimulate the economy. But many chose to pay off bills or put it into savings. My husband's vision of a nice robust savings account is the right one. But that doesn't mean I have to like it.

I didn't realize that I had been using purchases, money, or stuff to soothe my soul and to make me feel less guilty about not being at home. Thinking about spending and not doing it is still a battle, but one my husband has helped me to fight.

The Real Face of War

———— ✦ ————

I prayed for a man who was good with money and I got that. I didn't pray for a military man although I got that too. Patrick served in the U.S. Army for seven years. My brothers, brother-in-law, and sister-in-law are all retired from the military now, but in 2003 they were still serving our country. That's when we all read the headlines: "Pentagon readies huge force for Gulf." "Bush sick and tired of Iraq games." "War could be brief, planners say."

What the headlines should have also said is: "Career military man says goodbye to his wife and two children at 2 am."

That career military man is my brother-in-law Glenn and the wife is my sister Nicole. The two children are my nephew Jordan and niece Jasmine. This is the real face of Operation Enduring Freedom, of the war against terrorism and weapons of mass destruction. War protestors say peace is the answer, war supporters and warmongers say we have to strike now, or face the consequences of a madman bent on ridding the planet of the infidels. All I can think of is the sound of my nephew asking for his daddy and some potato chips for breakfast.

I called Nicole the night Glenn deployed, as well as the next morning. She told me my father had just called 15 minutes earlier to check on her. We tried not to cry. Our voices trembled and we used the silence to regain our composure. She has shed tears and so have I, but I knew if I cried it would break down the fortress she has delicately constructed around her feelings. So we talked, laughed and kept breathing deeply.

My father, who remembers his own deployment to Vietnam, had a different reaction. He wanted to know how much gear and equipment they were taking, and whether they were using a C-9 transport plane to travel. You could hear the pride and excitement in his voice. I know it's a man's way of dealing with emotion. Focus on the details and hardware instead of the tears.

Nicole says the daycare people are carrying out their own preemptive strike, having asked her some time ago if her husband would be among the soldiers shipping out. They want to be prepared for those children who, because they miss their parents, might begin acting out. We're glad they are thinking ahead. She told me that he had been on alert for a few weeks, so they knew eventually he would be called up. But it's never easy and she says while she's not afraid, she is very sad. He returned a week before Thanksgiving, after being away for three months attending drill sergeant school, and then off he went again.

I know there is a focus on the mechanics of war, the possible loss of life and the expensive tab that is left behind. But, never forget that there is a real face on every conflict. And it makes a difference when you know someone who is out there fighting for us, for our safety and way of life.

I know that reads like the latest military recruiting pamphlet, but my brother-in-law and the thousands like him, aren't reading the editorials or listening to a "Crossfire" debate on the merits of this war, or why we aren't going after North Korea. They just go where they are sent. They just follow orders. And their spouses, family and friends have to circle the wagons, hope for the best and wish them well.

That is what we did. We put our thoughts of the potential for tragedy, of the politics of the region, out of our heads and just threw our energy behind Nicole and her two children.

Military families like ours are used to times like this. We talk about duty stations and power of attorney. That week I used the words, "If God brought you to it, He'll bring you through it." I also told my sister to give the baby some potato chips for breakfast and to keep breathing. Everything will be all right.

Oprah's Hug

My parents have a picture of me that was taken backstage at the Fox Theatre. I was smiling and hugging Bill Cosby. While my husband and I have met a few famous people, I usually don't get to share those experiences with my sister or brothers. That changed during Oprah's 2003 seminar in St. Louis.

At the time, I was also a columnist at the St. Louis American Newspaper. A fellow writer had scored an interview with the talk show diva. After telling my colleague about my sister Nicole and her husband's story of deployment, she wanted to set up an interview with Nicole and Oprah. But that was the same weekend Nicole was supposed to graduate with her Master's in Psychology. It was during a three-way call with mom that she said, "Forget graduation, I want to see Oprah."

I wanted to go but hadn't purchased a ticket because of the price. "You know this is $185 bucks right?" They felt it would be a once in lifetime experience. "All right, I'm in."

This was an all-day conference and childcare still needed to be arranged. My husband would be working, my sister's husband is in the Middle East, my father didn't plan to come anywhere near the Oprah road show. What teenage girl wants to spend her entire Saturday watching four children, two, three, seven and eight years old? Only the best and most patient would do. Our 16-year-old niece took the job and we stocked up on snacks and double-checked the supply of band-aids. Warnings to the older cousins were issued and we felt free to leave the house at 8:30 that morning.

When we walked into America's Center, we spotted my colleague Cassandra right away. I saw her confer with someone official looking, then she came over and told my sister, "You get to meet her!" My sister's reply, "Meet who?" I wanted to check her pulse and call for a medic. She was whisked across the tape to the area set up for media and we waited. Then, 45 minutes later *she* arrived. She walked along the line of fans, gathered touching hands and stopped at me. We held hands for a full 90 seconds. (Yes, I counted.) I welcomed her to St. Louis, told her how great she looked, and expressed my anticipation for the day. She thanked me, checked on her beloved dogs, and continued down the line, eventually walking over for interviews. The first one up was Cassandra. She was given five minutes but fortunately got much more. When the time to introduce my sister came, my heart jumped into my throat. I watched my sister nod her head and say a few words. Her eyes got watery and she flashed her wonderful smile.

Then it happened. Oprah Winfrey gave her a big hug.

Oprah Winfrey in St. Louis
Oprah and My Sister Nicole

I could not believe what I was witnessing. The most powerful woman in television is hugging my sister. I had tears of joy. My heart felt full for Nicole. She had gone through so much that year—the loneliness, the fear, and the aching heart for her husband.

She deserved that hug from Oprah that day. And while everyone wants to know if I got to meet Ms. Winfrey, I quickly say, "Only briefly, but my sister got a hug, a pep talk and a photo." Oprah said to us that day, "Be so full of yourself that your cup runneth over." My sister's cup ran over and it certainly spilled on me.

Welcome Home!

————⌁————

After six months in Iraq, my brother-in-law Glenn returned home to his family safe and sound. You could hear the relief in my sister Nicole's voice.

The day before Glenn's scheduled arrival at the hanger on the Fort Still Oklahoma base, she said she was about to jump out of her skin with excitement. I asked her to take her cell phone with her to the welcoming ceremony and call me as soon as she spotted him. After no call came, I decided to call her cell phone instead. She answered the phone with an, "All is right with world tone in her voice." My immediate question, "Is he here?"

They had arrived at home just 10 minutes earlier. He could get two weeks to a month off after his turn in Operation Iraqi Freedom, but first the "in processing" must take place. All the equipment must be cleaned and logged and the troops themselves go through some sort of mental re-entry program. Can you imagine what it must be like? Your children have changed, you missed milestones, they missed you, and the family and house ran without you. They must feel so grateful to be home especially with so many murders of US troops still occurring.

And those troops returning home must also deal with the skepticism regarding the reason they were sent away from their families.

I come from a military family and I'm so thankful for the service of men and women in uniform. Nothing can shake the pride I have in the career my brother-in-law, my husband, my father, my brothers and my uncles chose. We all sacrificed.

I can't begin to know the heartache of those whose loved ones do not make it and the lifelong challenges faced by those who come home affected by their tours of duty.

To our heroes and their families, I salute you.

Mistaken Identity

My mother is really one of my heroes. She put up with so much from me but she never gave up on me. Being able to have a relationship with her today means I am constantly treated to her special brand of humor and the crazy situations she finds herself in. There was the time she sent Christmas cards but didn't realize they were in Spanish until I got one in the mail and called her!

My mother tells great stories. She'll often stop in the middle of a story to ask me, "Is this going to end up on the air or in one of your columns?" I usually say, "Tell me the rest and I'll let you know!" This mistaken identity story, I'm telling everyone about this!

It actually began with a frightening call from my father one weekend. "The police in your town just called to ask me if I owned a red Cadillac." Of course I wanted to know why, since my mother drives a red Cadillac and was sitting in our living room at the very moment. "Someone saw two distinguished black women in the front seat of a red Cadillac and two children with a white man in the back seat who looked like he was trying to hide." The caller questioned whether the women were being carjacked by the white man.

"Dad, you're kidding, right?" My father, who talks fast anyway, sped up the pace. "No, I'm, serious. The officer said some man saw the car and thought it looked suspicious." My reaction was a combination of amazement and frustration. My dad hadn't gotten the officer's name. Being a bit fearless and curious though, I called the police department to find out the deal.

My mother, sister, her husband and their two children had driven to see me for a visit. Apparently, during the trip from Fort Leonard Wood, while they were driving through St. Louis County, they attracted the attention of at least one man who was worried enough to contact the police.

The dispatcher who answered the phone knew exactly what I was talking about and put the officer who'd called my father on the phone. The officer said the man (or rather an "itty-bitty" man as he described him), spotted the car in Missouri, on I-44 and Lindbergh Boulevard, felt something might be wrong, and followed my mother and sister into Illinois. About five minutes from our house, the man spotted a patrol car and flagged it down. The officer called in the license plate number, and with the information in hand, called my father and asked if he owned such a vehicle. I was speechless and confused on so many levels. The officer said that from talking to the man, they felt he might be the type to exaggerate things but they wanted to be safe, so they ran the plates.

Okay. I was astounded. Let me take a breath here and finish the story.

What they thought was a kidnapping was actually a homecoming. The two black women in the front seat were Mom and Nicole. The white man in the back seat who looked like he was hiding was my brother-in-law Glenn. He is black but has been confused for Hispanic or Italian, never white. He says he spent much of the trip as a referee between his son and daughter in the back seat. My sister and mother got a kick out of being called "distinguished black women" but wondered why the man followed them for 20 some-odd 20 minutes. The police officer said they get this kind of thing every now and then and do try to check things out.

How do you react to such a thing when the itty-bitty man in question thinks black women are in harm's way and a white man is the culprit? That's quite the twist on profiling in the U.S. isn't it? While my brother-in-law was shaking his head all afternoon at the notion that he was a suspicious white man, perhaps my mother's reaction was the best. She said, "I'm tired of people thinking my Cadillac is red, it's actually cranberry."

Weddings, Cousins and Long Drives

My parents have been married for 54 years. They fuss at each other but you can feel the love. I am definitely a romantic and I love weddings! Getting to watch my sister-in-law Martha marry her groom Greg was truly romantic.

His eyes never left hers. He held her hands throughout the ceremony and choked up a bit when reciting his vows. Her big brother, my husband, walked her down the aisle and responded to the minister, who asked, "Who gives this woman in holy matrimony?"

"My family and I do," said Patrick. Her vows were said in an unwavering and clear tone. The kiss was delicate. One strap of her wedding dress slipped and he gently lifted it back up before photos were taken.

Sounds like a romance novel, doesn't it? It looked like one, too. Martha and Greg got married in the mountains of Tennessee. It was a beautiful day for two families to become one.

We drove to the wedding, eight hours in all. I packed the usual snacks, DVDs, books, and too many clothes for the weekend. I was excited to see my husband's family again. Today's families are so spread out and my husband's is no different. My mother-in-law and brother-in-law live in St. Croix. Martha was stationed in Korea at the time and now lives in San Antonio. Their sister, Albina, lives in Atlanta with her family.

It's natural for women like me to go to a wedding and think about their own wedding and marriage. I was thinking of the years Patrick and I had spent together making each other crazy, striving, regrouping and going for the goal line. I couldn't help but think about all the things I would have done differently at my wedding.

For one, I advise to never plan your wedding yourself if you can help it, especially if you live in one city and the wedding is in another! I lost weight from the stress and had to have my wedding dress taken in three times. And a wedding planner would never have allowed friends to sit in the two front rows that should have been reserved for family! A wedding planner also would have ensured that the song played for the first dance, as husband and wife would NOT have started with the line, "So you're having my baby!" You read that correctly. When we heard the song, we almost fell over from embarrassment. I looked dead at my parents, who luckily were oblivious to the lyrics.

And a wedding planner would likely have given us better directions to our honeymoon site—Memphis. As it was, my father, in his special way, said, "Girl, this is what you do: You take highway so-and-so and then go left for a few hours and you should be there in no time." It took so much longer than he claimed, so long that we arrived at 3 am. Despite a reservation, the hotel had given our suite away. Funny thing is, the clerk didn't tell us the room we were being given was not the same size suite as we'd booked. I only realized this after we walked by another room being cleaned and noticed the size difference right way. A brief and cordial conversation with the manager led to an up-grade, two complimentary nights and a free jazz brunch. Years later, I am still laughing about my father's directions.

I love weddings, in part, because I love LOVE. But marriage takes more than that. We know that now, but when we were driving hours out of our way to get to that honeymoon suite, all we could think about was our love. Years later, we still think about our love. But now it comes between thoughts of health insurance costs, college entrance exams, oil changes, parent-teacher conferences, laundry and pumpkin carving.

So here's a toast to all those who love LOVE, and make it work.

Strength of Character

My husband has done two things most of the American public will never do. He has started his own business, and he has worn dreadlocks. However, in the summer of 2005, I cut off his beautiful locks.

It was something I was hoping to avoid but that I knew was inevitable. One Friday evening after a particularly hot day, he had had enough and asked me to go get the scissors.

He had asked me to cut his dreadlocks several times before. I just refused to do so. I loved his hair. It was so strong, and it made him look even more handsome than he already did.

But, he is a practical man, and he explained to me that, while he worked outside as a landscaper and lawn care expert, the heat on those thick locks was often overwhelming. He had to wear a bandana to keep the dust and grass out of his hair, creating even more heat on his head. And, whenever he got them re-twisted, he had to set aside four or more hours.

I did manage to pout my way into getting him to keep them for another year. But, I knew in the end he would have to do what he wanted and needed to do.

What neither of us counted on was how different he would look and the reaction from friends and our family.

We are members at New Life in Christ Interdenominational Church, in Lebanon, Illinois. I remember that following Sunday, dozens of members, including our pastor, Dr. Dudley, stopped dead in their tracks, did double takes and let Patrick know how different he looked or how good they thought the locks had looked on him.

The reaction really took him aback. He was shocked. I was surprised that he was shocked. I thought he knew that most people thought they looked beautiful.

However, as most black women can attest, people of different ethnic groups often feel right at home commenting on our hair, "How do you get your hair like that?"

You can imagine the reaction to dreadlocks. "Do you wash them?" "Don't they smell?" One woman even reached out and touched his hair once with a look of minor disgust on her face. So he had all that in mind and more when he decided to shed them.

But, in the Virgin Islands, where my husband was born, many conservative parents (his included) did not allow their children to wear dreadlocks, not wanting them to embrace the Rastafarian movement that endorsed smoking ganja as a religious rite.

Right after I cut off Patrick's locks, a funny thing happened. He missed them as much as I did and began the process of growing them back. Today, he has a full head of locks again and they are beautiful. To me, even Patrick's locks have character.

Can You Quit Your Job?

When Our Sons Were Young
Marcus and PJ

I hope my sons will grow into men who have their father's character, which begins with his work ethic! He is the hardest-working man I know, only after my father. But there are days I just don't know. Most mornings, like most parents, I grab my cattle prod and herd my sons through the morning routine of showers, hair grease, clothes and breakfast, watching the clock and the street for the school bus. Some mornings are easier than others, but most rank as your run-of-the mill challenge.

One day in 2006, things took a strange turn. PJ, at

age 10, was happily distracted by the sunshine as he reflected on what the school day had in store. It was the day called "specials," when students go to library, gym and take computer and music classes. Who among you wouldn't look forward to those days?

But another issue distracted then six-year-old Marcus. "Are you coming home early?"

It's the one question that I still get from Marcus every other day. And it's a question that makes me cringe a bit inside. How do I explain to him that I'll try my hardest, but that working in a newsroom means much of my schedule is not under my control? How do I explain to him that being able to be with them in the morning means coming home later at night?

I had tried to explain in the past. That day, he delivered a blow that left me breathless. "Mommy, can you quit your job?"

The only words I could utter were, "Can I what?"

"Can you quit your job?" And as if that wasn't enough, he added, "Can you quit your job and stay home with me?" I took a deep breath and began my verbal tap dance.

"Sweetie, you aren't even home during the day. You're in school. And by working, I get paid, and with that money, we pay for the car and food and trips to *Blockbuster*."

I believe it was the reference to his beloved movie

rentals that got him. "Okay," he said, "Keep working then."

A part of me does want to be a stay-at-home mom and spend my days volunteering at area charities, going to the gym and mopping my kitchen floor every day. But the other part of me likes to work.

I thought, too, of the many women who have no choice but to work hard, holding down several jobs. I'm sure those women would love to stay home, if only they could afford it.

Those were issues I couldn't explain to my six-year-old then. But I'll bet he'd still like me to stay home or at least change my hours to be home earlier.

Memorable Career Moments

Right: Missouri
History Museum
Ruby Dee and Me

Left: Fox Theatre
Patrick, Bill
Cosby and Me

Right: McKendree
University
Dr. Maya Angelou
and Me

57

Grandpa the Tour Guide

Grandpa Isiah and Marcus Relaxing

Our sons may not have me coming home at 3 pm but they have their grandparents — something I wish I'd had. During the summer of 2006, the boys and I drove two hours down Interstate 44 to see my parents near Fort Leonard Wood where my dad retired over 30 years ago. We stayed up late talking and watching movies. Saturday, we slept in and ate breakfast at noon. My father took PJ and Marcus fishing that afternoon and came back with stories and six catfish (yuck)! PJ headed straight for the shower to get the "fish smell" off his body. Marcus wore the smell like a badge of honor. He was as happy as I'd ever seen him. That afternoon, we went to a park in the small downtown. Growing up, I'd only gone there a few times. My father and I sat on a park bench while the boys climbed and crawled at a nearby playground. Then we headed toward a walking/biking trail along the Rubidoux River. My father described the history of the trout spring while the boys threw rocks into the clear water. It was another place I'd never gone while growing up.

Then it hit me. I said, "I've got to see my old high school!" My enthusiasm was totally lost on the boys who weren't nearly as excited as I was. Wouldn't you know it? My old high school is now the middle school, and the new high school has an elevator! My offspring weren't interested at all; they just wanted to play some more.

Much to my retired military father's delight, those same children who didn't care a bit about my old high school were more than willing to let their grandfather take them to a military museum with him as our tour guide. He showed his grandsons a bit of what it was like for him in Korea and Vietnam. They were especially thrilled to see the type of bridges he once helped build, the type of weapons he used in the '50s and '60s and of course, the explosives. Go figure!

For about 48 hours, we hung out in my small hometown without a shopping mall or amusement park in sight. I was secretly hoping that PJ and Marcus learned that it doesn't take a great deal of money to have a good vacation. I was also hoping those precious hours with their grandfather would become lifelong memories. He was so busy serving in the military when I was growing up that he had little time for movie nights, fishing trips and museum tours. I missed growing up with my own grandparents. I only have a few faint memories of my father's father, sitting in a rocking chair with his legs crossed, smoking a pipe. I do remember the food, the farm and the big beds with what seemed like 50 pounds of quilts. The only words I remember my grandfather saying as he slowly rocked were, "Yes, Lord."

My two boys will have far more memories than that. They don't realize it yet, but they are so fortunate to be able to see and hear from that generation. And I know my parents are living every mother and father's dream, to see their grandchildren grow up. I want them to pass along their stories of being stationed in Germany and getting there not on an airplane, but on a ship. I want PJ and Marcus to realize that there was a time when people they know didn't get hundreds of dollars worth of Christmas presents, but instead a handmade doll, candy and a piece of fruit. I want their grandparents to tell these children of privilege that their sacrifice is the very reason they can live as they do today! I pray that they get the message.

I Could Be Bitter

——————⌇——————

All I ever wanted was to be a wife and mother. I had visions about what type of mother I would be. I'd bake cookies and volunteer at their schools! I've done those things, and I've seen the contrast between intentional parenting and those caught up in the system. It's heart breaking.

On one Saturday afternoon, I spoke to dozens of girls at a juvenile detention center. I did not get to know their individual stories, but I could see that many had difficulty and trying times written all over them. Then that evening, my family attended our oldest son's first piano recital.

It was such a sad and stark contrast that many times during the evening I wondered if I'd said anything that might uplift the girls I'd seen that day. I wondered if any of my words, jokes, admonition or wisdom had made a dent in the carefully constructed shields they had to carry. The other half of the evening, I spent smiling so deeply, I actually felt warmer. I knew that my son was terrified to be in front of more than a hundred people playing "Surfboard Boogie" for the first time in public. So, I prayed that he would be confident and make it through the two-and-a-half-minute piece. And I hoped that he would do so without breaking down, or worse yet, crying as I'd heard many students had done in the past. There were nearly 30 students. I kept thinking of the girls, though. What if their parents had been able to provide a stable home and upbringing? Wouldn't they be at a piano recital too? Or maybe they'd be at a spelling bee or a softball tournament or SOMETHING other than foster care and juvenile court.

I could blame many people because there is certainly enough blame to go around. The easy access to drugs and guns and addiction; the lack of quality jobs, affordable healthcare and housing; and the failure of urban education are all hurdles to creating stable families and healthy children. I looked at the girls, and I thought of then Senator Obama's fateful comment about those who are bitter and cling to guns and religion. I was looking at girls who could easily be bitter, square in their faces. They've been abused and left behind. They are hurt and angry. And what are they clinging to?

I walked into the Saturday sunshine thinking that I didn't know a thing about the real pain that institutionalized girls and boys and their mothers and fathers are facing. All over the country there are residential treatment facilities and juvenile detention centers. Some are state-run and others are not-for-profit. There are thousands of foster families who step in when parents willingly or unwillingly have their children taken away. There are heroes in the foster care system, and there are those who are not. There are court advocates, counselors, judges and many others who are all that's left for some of the girls and boys to cling to.

They have to fight the past hurts and tragedies to not become bitter while others simply make the choice to be bitter. And I do understand that SOME of that bitterness is over jobs lost overseas, the mortgage crisis and the other social battles we face. But honestly, even if you're watching your paycheck shrink and your bills grow, I'd hope that you could put your bitterness aside if you had the chance to see the faces of the girls I saw that Saturday afternoon.

In This House

When Patrick and I use the phrase, "In this house," it means the foundation or principles we believe our sons should have as children of ours. It's the way we behave and perform in life. We want them to leave our care knowing how to clean and cook, how to handle money, how to control themselves, and how to work.

The statement I don't want them to ever say is, "My parents didn't talk to me about...my parents didn't teach me how to..." We are training, we are pruning and we fertilizing, uplifting, providing and encouraging them. We are trying to do those things even when it's difficult, and it's usually difficult. Pruning is the worst. You never really get the whole thorn. The pointy dangerous part may be gone, but you can still see where it used to be. We are not perfect parents by any stretch of the imagination, but we are actively trying. And I can tell our children know it because they roll their eyes when we launch into yet another discussion of what they need to know and who we want them to be when they leave "*this house*."

So many families are not growing up with their relatives close by, so they are missing out on the type of wisdom once shared between generations about how to raise children. Many of us find ourselves relying on our friends.

So let me provide a few conversation starters and relationship builders. If nothing else, they might spark an exchange. We know our children, our teens especially, don't really want advice or think they need it, but it's our responsibility as parents and adults to say what needs to be said. If we don't share with them, who will? These are some things I would like young ladies and young men to know.

Young Ladies:

1. Focus on your health (physical and emotional) more than you focus on your image.

2. Look with suspicion upon the image of women in pop culture. You do not need, as Usher sings, "Hair falling down to your waist." You do not need 5-inch heels or $500 shoes. You do not need an expensive purse to be a woman of value.

3. Answer for yourself what it means to be a "good woman."

4. Please know that all men are not dogs.

5. If you want to be in a relationship, make sure you are ready to be in a relationship.

6. Keep your legs closed.

7. Education will lead to the ability to fulfill your destiny and pay the rent or mortgage.

8. Do not go into debt for things that don't appreciate in value. Pay your debt monthly. If you can't, don't use plastic.

Young Men:

1. Ignore many of the images of young men in pop culture.

2. Get a new understanding of what it means to respect yourself.

3. The world needs you to be strong and self-assured more than you know.

4. Keep your pants up, as it relates to fashion and intimacy.

5. You have skill, intelligence, gifts and contributions that must be revealed and nurtured. Ask for a mentor.

6. When a woman asks, "Where are all the good men?" live your life so that you'll be able to say, "Here I am!"

7. Education will lead to the ability to fulfill your destiny and pay the rent or mortgage.

8. Do not go into debt for things that don't appreciate in value. Pay your debt monthly. If you can't, don't use plastic.

Norbit ~ Not A Bit

————— ❧ —————

I want to be clear that I'm neither a supermom nor a film critic. I am struggling to keep a lid on things, as my sons grow taller and more independent. Monitoring everything they read, watch and hear is more difficult than you could imagine.

Last year my youngest wanted to watch a movie trailer on television about a horror film as I was trying to get him to go to bed. It was a trailer for the horror flick "The Possession." It's about a girl who discovered an antique box at a yard sale that doesn't contain old war letters, but an ancient and yes, evil spirit. Count me out!

I have no intention of ever watching another horror film. I have a history of walking out of movie theaters and with ticket prices so high, why waste the money? Actually, I only walked out of two movies. The first time was in 1980 when Jack Nicholson starred in "The Shining." I have since seen the entire thing but in the comfort of my home. I just don't like to be scared. But walking out of a movie for any other reason is something I had never done until the Eddie Murphy film, "Norbit." Why I thought this film would be anything like "The Nutty Professor," is beyond me. I knew it had a PG-13 rating. The Motion

Picture Association of America was wrong. From the 15 minutes I saw, "Norbit" clearly should have been rated R. I am so thankful that the theater management gave us all of our money back and commented that we weren't the first to walk out.

The profanity, sexual content and use of endearing terms for women as b—h and other disgusting, harsh expressions for women, along with obese black people came flying out immediately. I kept thinking it would get better, but it didn't. My oldest son actually excused himself and went to the bathroom to escape the images on the screen. I had to apologize to them and explain that I thought the movie was going to be funny. Boy, was I wrong. And to an adult audience it was probably funny, but not funny enough for me.

I know it's comedy. I know it's only a movie, and I know that it's personal taste. But come on! I don't even have a problem with Tyler Perry donning a wig and a floral housecoat to play Madea. It's not about that. And I've seen Martin Lawrence get into the fat suit a time or two, and I laughed. But "Norbit" takes the genre to a new level, and it's not a higher level.

And I don't even have enough space to go off about why the obese black woman had to have the ugly name, Raspusia, and the equally ugly disposition while the love of Norbit's life is the thin and beautiful one. I know, I know, there are plenty of evil skinny women and it's supposed to be comedy, but there were more than a few gasps of disbelief and moments of uncomfortable silence in the theater when some of the dialogue was being delivered. I want to believe that we've turned the corner on black exploitation films that feature caricatures of us, but this might as well have been released in Vaudeville.

And it's especially sad for Eddie Murphy and his "Dream Girls" Academy Award nomination. I believe he lost because the Foreign Press Corps saw Norbit and decided to hold a grudge and its nose.

I messed up by taking my sons to something like this. The really sad part to me is that several other parents who also brought children that night stayed in the theater, and I even heard from one parent who said, "My kids loved it." By and large, Hollywood still thinks the black experience is limited to certain characters and situations. There are many breakouts and breakthroughs, but "Norbit"...that's a setback.

I'm Whining

I've learned one thing after my dream of motherhood came true: it's exhausting! There is only one time of the year that I really wish I had a different career. Summertime. The months of June, July and August make me want to leave my year-round 30-year broadcasting career behind in the dust and run at breakneck speed toward the holy grail of nine-month careers – TEACHING!

No matter how old I get, the image of summer reminds me of the most wonderful words in any child's language, "SCHOOL'S OUT!" The last bell would ring, and we would run out of the school into the waiting sunshine, only looking back to see the empty hallways and perhaps to take one last look at our lockers.

Now that I'm a working mother, my only connection to summer is to make arrangements for summer camp. My schedule? Let's see: Monday-work; Tuesday-work; Wednesday-work; Thursday-work; Friday-work; Saturday-think about last week's work; Sunday-think about next week's work. Looking at the calendar makes me feel a little old, but still very happy my children get to experience another, "SCHOOL'S OUT!"

I know it sounds like I'm whining. Well, I am. I am absolutely whining. I mean, I love my career. I truly enjoy making a living and providing for my family and myself. But I really miss feeling the emotional high that kids get as they anticipate the last day of school—no more homework, no more classes, no more projects and no more tests, if only for three months.

The only feeling that comes close is the attitude I have just days before a great vacation. Christmas in San Antonio comes to mind. I was just plain giddy as the Texas trip approached. I was so excited to be getting away. I was thrilled to be able to see my sister, sisters-in-law and an uncle, all in one trip. I was going to a city I'd never been to, and I was going to be away from work for an entire week. We've taken cruises, driven halfway across country and done the "staycation," but a trip to San Antonio was just what Santa ordered.

My sister-in-law, Martha, was an incredible hostess. She doesn't miss a detail. Even the soap in her guest bathroom made me feel like I was staying at a resort. The weather was just right. Not too hot and not too cold, especially since it was December. The River Walk and the Alamo were exciting and interesting sights to see. It was great to be a tourist in such a wonderful place.

Sometimes I wonder if my excitement over vacations or time off is an indication of something else. I'm sure it's not, but it seems, as I get older, vacations take on a different level of importance. It may have everything to do with the fact that my husband works, I work and our children work (in school). Our time together is naturally limited by those schedules. So, getting time away together is important.

Who doesn't love a vacation, other than workaholics? My love may also have something to do with the aging process...of my children. My 16-year-old has had absolutely no desire to go with me to the grocery store or any store for years now. I remember the time when he wouldn't miss an opportunity to stroll up and down the aisles with me. As he entered adolescence, he pulled away. Marcus is still pretty willing to go anywhere with me. My husband calls us Shopper One and Shopper Two. The boys do love vacations, but unlike me during my childhood, they ask questions like, "Which hotel are we staying in?" and, "What time is the flight?"

The only question I asked as a child before we took a summer vacation was...actually, I never asked any questions because we all knew where we were going, where we were staying and when we were leaving - 4 o'clock in the morning. That's what we knew about summer vacations. I could still become a teacher and have my summers off, but soon enough my children will be off to college, Patrick and I will be working on retirement and we'll have the entire year to ourselves. I guess I can handle my 12-month career until then!

Give a Sister a Chance

When he was 15, I had a conversation with my son PJ about dating because I decided that as his mother, I should speak my mind regarding the issue of the type of girls I felt he should go out with. I knew I was stepping into delicate territory and could even completely turn him off, but I couldn't hold back.

The one thing I had no plans to say to him was, "Only date black girls." I just told him my story from my heart. I didn't marry his father until we were 31. I told him that I felt afraid that I would never meet the right man for me because there were so few men like his father. I gave him some statistics. I told him about black men in jail. About black boys dropping out of school, and I told him there are more black women in college than black men. And I told him what that meant, that there are fewer educated, stable black men available and that was the reality that I faced.

As his eyes appeared to glaze over, I told him that as a black woman, I knew that the pickins were slim. I wanted to be crystal clear with him, so I emphasized that I do not feel that I am better than a Caucasian, Asian or Latina woman. We just have slightly different cultures. There is something to be said for collard greens, challah, schnitzel, huevos rancheros, or dim sum - for culture.

I hadn't lost him yet, so I continued by telling him that all relationships are hard and that he has to find someone he is compatible with, someone who values the same things he does. But knowing how hard it was for me to find his father, I asked him to do what may sound like a crazy thing. I asked my son to *give a sister a chance*. Yes, I basically asked him not to overlook the black girls in his school.

This issue has been in the back of my mind since that sunny day in May 2002, when my son brought home a phone number given to him by a little girl in his kindergarten class. She had bouncy blonde ringlets and was adorable. Let's call her Amy. I was still shaking my head weeks later.

I had just gotten home from work when he ran up to me, gave me a hug and pulled a little torn slip of paper out of his pocket. It was about half the size of a stick of gum.

"Guess what Amy gave me?"

"What?" I asked, without the slightest clue that everyone in the room was about to age.

"Amy gave me her phone number." The innocence in his voice was only overshadowed by his excitement, as if he'd won a prize. I realized that I needed to say something instead of just standing there staring at the slip of paper.

"Why? I mean, what did she say when she gave you the number?" Now you know I was holding my breath, waiting for his response.

"Nothing. She just said she wanted to give it to me."

I wanted to know if he had given her his phone number in exchange, and he said no. I can't say I was relieved to find out that he hadn't because it would be just a matter of time before numbers are exchanged and dates are made.

If I ever doubted it, this touching scene confirmed that I was officially a member of the "older generation." As my son was looking at me with wide eyes, waiting for me to say something or give him permission to watch more cartoons, I was thinking, *Now, when I was six years old...* And then I thought, *Will my son be pursued by adorable girls with bouncy blonde curls?*

Flash forward, and I realize that many teens feel freer to date whomever they want. Perhaps we can credit MTV for that. And as crazy as it sounds, I want my son to feel (mostly) free to date whomever he wants to as well. But try as I might, I can't get away from the never-ending stream of negative headlines about black men, fatherless boys, dropout rates, baby mama drama, poverty rates and incarceration. Who will turn those headlines around? God blessed me with two sons that my husband and I can shape, prune and nurture into fine young men and husbands. Our boys can do their part.

I know not everyone agrees with me. I've even been told that I can't tell them who to date. I'm sticking to my motherly guns on this one. I just want girls who look like me to have a chance with my sons who look just like them. I want them, at their tender ages, to somehow understand that even in this day of rapidly changing technology and rapidly changing social cues, that there is something bigger than their personal desires. I actually believe as a parent, that I can encourage and direct each of them to decide to be that black man who is not only purposeful about college and his career, but also is purposeful about his girlfriend and, ultimately, his wife. A colleague once told me he felt we couldn't save urban schools until we saved the black family. I truly believe that my decision is a part of the solution to stabilizing and saving the black community.

I didn't tell him this, but as black women have long battled images of beauty that don't include them, I hope to open his eyes to see girls who look like me, his mother and actually see beauty and not be swayed by music, commercials, television and movies to believe otherwise. I know how meaningful it is to have my husband look at me and know all of who I am. The experience of having Patrick understand and relate is irreplaceable. My heart hurts at the thought of all the black boys and black men being lost and all the black women left to grieve what could have been.

I remember during my pregnancy thinking that I was carrying a man, a black man. I dreamed several times about seeing him as a grown man. I was standing across a street from him, and I couldn't see his face. In the dream he was waving goodbye to me. It was clear that he had grown into a good man, and I was so proud of him. It was always the same in that dream. He was waving goodbye and turning to walk away from me, but I was proud of him. This is much more complicated than I can explain here. But I will be proud of him no matter his choice. I know all I can do is make suggestions. I know that love blooms in the most unexpected places. But I also know that for all the single black women yearning for an honorable, solid black man, I have to do my part as a mother to raise just that. I was one of those women, and I used to wonder, *Who raised these men I was encountering?*

After my speech ended, PJ gave me no argument, and didn't ask any questions. He also didn't roll his eyes and look disgusted or annoyed. Of course, I have no idea what the future holds. But I feel I did my job. The seed has been planted.

Puppy Kisses

I am one of those women who has never had a problem telling her age, and I still don't. But now I feel the passage of time. All I have to do is look at my sons and see time has flown by!

My son PJ, now 16, is about to get his driver's license. I seem to talk every other day about the short time he has left before he packs up his life, and our car, and heads to college. I remember his first day of kindergarten. How I cried after taking him to the bus stop.

He's the one that used to give me what he called "puppy kisses," the one who created a song for me, "I Love My Pomp Peep." He's the one who used to run across the room when I got home from work, jump into my arms and yell, "Mommy's home, Mommy's home!"

Okay, enough of the melodrama. Okay, maybe a little more of the melodrama. Even buying school supplies is emotional for me these days. I've always enjoyed shopping for school supplies. I love the smell of fresh paper in the morning! But I do go overboard. Did he really need five bottles of Elmer's glue when the list only called for two? But now the question is, does he really need a $100 calculator and an $80 backpack with padding for a laptop and slots for headphones? And what about a $125 pair of running shoes for cross country?

School supplies aren't what they used to be when I was growing up. I remember getting my bag of gold home, dumping the contents on my bed and surveying them one by one, even smelling the paper. When I was able, I would write my name on each and every tablet.

Those days are gone. Now even his Honors Algebra book is online, and his little brother has opted to get his Social Studies book online. Emailing homework, creating power points and downloading homework onto flash drives - all that's commonplace for these boys.

But I don't want to forget how it all began. I remember my husband shouting, "Yes, Yes!" at my flat stomach, after I walked him to the bathroom and showed him the positive home pregnancy test. And I'll never forget the look of wonder on PJ's face when I walked him into class on his first day of kindergarten. Let me admit that I put him on the bus because I wanted him to have that experience on his first day. Then I walked home, got in my car and followed the bus to school to meet him at the classroom door. Don't judge!

In two short years, I'll add to the memories. Prom, graduation, college acceptance letters and dorm move in day. He'll stand tall. He'll smile that shy smile, take his diploma and maybe, just maybe, he'll look for us in the audience. I'll voice the latest in a long line of prayers for his education and his future. "Lord, please let him be a man of excellence, please let him have amazing professors and please let this not be the end of puppy kisses and the Pomp Peep song."

About Being Married

Relationships have always been hard. I'm sure that you have found some things in my stories, which are much like your own, the struggles, revelations and the triumphs. Embrace what you have, and be willing to work through your relationships.

Bringing awareness to where you are, and where you are not will allow conversations, healing and solutions. We have to talk about it because too many of us are not doing that.

To Husbands:

1. Your wife needs to hear your words.

2. Your wife needs to know when you are in pain, confused and frustrated.

3. Your wife needs to know your dreams so that she can help you in achieving them.

4. Your wife needs to know that you cherish her.

To Wives:

1. Your husband can't read your mind.

2. Your husband doesn't always know how to handle your emotions.

3. Your husband may show love differently than you do. Figure it out.

Married Couples:

1. Don't stop talking to one another.

2. Spend time doing something together. You don't even have to leave the house.

3. Do not complain about each other to other people, especially your mother/your family.

4. Be brave enough to explain your needs to your spouse. Start with "I," not "you."

5. Drop "never" and "always" from your vocabulary in negative references.

6. Kiss, hold hands and never stop flirting with each other.

Crossing Male Boundaries

———— ᐁᐧᑐ ————

I have always thought of myself as a helpful sort of person. I mean, I have taken my own advice! I hold the door open for the elderly, I correct my sons' grammar and I let other motorists into traffic. But I know that my help isn't always welcome or necessary, especially when I don't really know what I'm doing.

Consider the time my husband and neighbor were installing a new doorframe on our patio door. It took them a day and a half and tools I'd never even seen before. These men know their way around a tool chest, and there isn't much work in the home that they can't do. So it was with that knowledge that I decided to take on a task normally reserved for my husband's expert attention. I decided to cut our son's hair...

I know, I know. I should have left well enough alone. But my husband was so busy, and I just wanted to help him out. And the boys really needed a haircut. I mean, there comes a time when the best brush and hair grease can't hide the look of a boy in need of a set of clippers. So knowing my efforts might end in disaster, I ushered the little man cubs upstairs to the bathroom and pulled Patrick's clippers out of their big case and set to work.

I knew that I was in trouble right away, but *Hey!* I thought, *I can fix it...just a little more off over here and here. Oh, Lord. NO!*

It's still funny to me because at the time, I thought it would be easy. I said to myself, *How hard can it be? Just glide the clippers over the hair, and it's a done deal.* I've watched many a barber take those clippers, hold the cord in one hand and just fly over heads. My husband had always cut PJ and Marcus' hair and made it look easy. That's how experts do things, they make it look easy. It actually takes great skill. And yes, my friends, it's skill I don't have.

I also learned that most people have lumpy heads. From far away, your head looks smooth, but up close with clippers in hand, you'll discover so many twists and turns and lumps and crevices, you wonder how the brain inside is doing. But I thought I could just sit the clippers on those adorable heads and glide them around and create this Grammy-night, magazine hairstyle. What I created was children with hair so jagged and uneven, I had to quickly tell on myself so my husband could clean up my mess.

Patrick was calm when he saw what I'd done to our offspring. He shook his head and said, "What did you do?" I felt like an 11-year-old who tried to cook and succeeded only in wasting eggs, milk, flour and leaving a mess for the real chef to clean up. Clean it up he did in no time flat. He took the clippers in one hand, the cord in the other and ten minutes later, you'd never have known I had been anywhere near their hair or the male boundary.

Happy Anniversary!

A Night On the Town
Patrick and Me

Patrick and I have just clocked 18 years together, 19 if you count the time I chased him. I mean, the time we dated. I remember my outcry to the Lord, "Lord, please bring me someone to love, someone who would better me, who liked some of the same things I did!" I met Patrick a few months later. I embarrass him when I talk about our first date, his piano hands, his quiet way, his perfectly gorgeous...okay, okay I really need to stop right there.

Marriage is never easy, but we have been blessed to learn so much about how to make it work. Listening is better than talking, understanding is better than listening, and compassion and patience are even better than understanding. And as one sister-in-law told me before I got married, "Girl, there may be times he'll get on your nerves so bad, even his breathing will be irritating." But you have to get over that. As actress Ruby Dee told me regarding her book, *"My One Good Nerve,"* and her 50-year marriage to Ossie Davis, "Yes, he gets on my nerves, but that didn't stop me from loving him."

Celebrating our anniversary each year, I reflect on the times it was harder than I ever thought it would be. The times I didn't know if we would make it. I think about all the long conversations we've had—okay, let's call them arguments. I think about the realization that this was not a greeting card. And that we were two very different people who some-how fell in love, stayed in love and stayed married.

I'll admit, I love a good party, but what I love even more, is being able to say, "I love you Patrick. We worked it out." I'm happy to say that we are still jumping over hurdles, grazing a few while running hand in hand. And I do still love his piano hands and his kiss me lips...okay, okay, I'll stop right here, again.

Miracles Do Happen

Whoever thinks of serious health issues early in your marriage? I know I didn't. So when the doctor told me, "arthritis of the spine," I was in shock. I was getting my hair done after having an MRI the previous week. I had been in such pain for weeks. I was popping Ibuprofen like they were breath mints. There was no comfortable position to sit or sleep. Heating pads didn't help. Knowing I couldn't keep taking pain pills, I called my doctor who scheduled the MRI. He thought it might be a pinched nerve or a bulging disc, which made me think of steroid shots, and worse, surgery.

I'd had two babies, two miscarriages and multiple root canals. But this was pain like nothing I'd ever experienced. Surgery and shots in my back? I wasn't ready for that. Nor was I ready to hear arthritis of the spine either. Before I even had the MRI, the office staff called with a few questions about insurance and whether or not I had claustrophobia. For a split second, I thought of saying yes to ensure I would be in an open MRI. But that would be a lie.

What they should have asked me was, "How much do you weigh?" Oh, I fit in the tube, but barely. I spent so much time thinking of how much more weight I'd have to gain to NOT fit in the tube that I wasn't really focused on how close my face was to the top, how little room there was to squirm, and how much my back was starting to really hurt in that position. It took almost an hour. I could not wait to get out and get home. I'm feeling a little stomach ache just writing these words!

It's sort of strange that hearing bad news is only compounded by having to tell others. I called my husband, crying, to let him know what the test showed. I couldn't believe what I heard. I didn't even understand what it meant. I wondered what was going to happen to me. *Was I going to have this type of pain the rest of my life?* I didn't want surgery. I simply wanted to go back to sleeping, sitting and standing like a normal person. But Patrick had that loving "get a grip" voice.

He told me it was going to be all right. I know he believed it.

But nothing prepared me for my youngest son's reaction. I didn't tell him the diagnosis, but he knew I had been in pain for a while. He asked me, "Mom, do you have any of your blessed water left?" Our church had recently held a revival, and the visiting Bishop asked that we bring water to the altar for the duration of the revival, saying there were many miracles in the Bible-related to water. At the end of the week, we were told to drink it, to use it however sparingly and report the results. One of my dear friends asked me the same thing but added, "What are you waiting for?"

For some reason, I had been saving mine for something big! Arthritis of the spine is surely big.

I prayed for healing, and that Saturday night I drank a cup of the blessed water. Sunday morning, I remember waking up and thinking immediately, *I don't feel any pain, I don't feel any pain!* I was able to get out of bed without any struggle, and I haven't felt any pain since.

My doctor and the physical therapist did tell me that I needed to check my work environment. Was my computer too high, causing me to look up? Was my chair too high, causing my feet to swing? Was the computer too far away, causing me to lean forward and slouch? I had two out of three, including a habit of raising my shoulders due to tension. Even after drinking the blessed water, I made those changes to my office. I'm so thankful for the miracle, and I am wise enough to know better than to ignore good advice.

Addicted to Grocery Stores

Hi, my name is Carol Daniel, and I'm addicted to grocery stores!

If there were such a support group, complete with ten steps, I'd be among the first to join. I can lovingly blame my mother because she has the gene; it's in her DNA. We just love to explore grocery stores, especially when we're out of town! My husband doesn't get it. Of course, he's a hunter. Know the prey, stalk the prey, bag the prey and bring the prey home. I'm not that kind of hunter. I'm a looker, toucher, stroller and gatherer. Set out for a certain prey, but being mindful that there may be other prey, (on sale or in new packaging) warranting a second look. There have been times when nearly every aisle was to be explored because each might yield some previously unknown treasure!

In today's economy and with today's waistline, I'm striving to streamline. I want to show my children that planning and self-control are good and that waste is bad. I read somewhere that as consumers, we waste 30 percent of the vegetables we buy! Now that's just, well, wasteful! I finally bought a graduated shelf for my spices because I was tired of coming home around Thanksgiving with yet another container of allspice! And I spent three hours cleaning out the refrigerator because I was tired of not knowing what I had in there. And I was tired of knowing that what I did have was likely to be too old to consume. Or it might be one of those, "let's try this," that turned out to be, "I'll never buy that again."

And believe me, I've just about tried it all before. Like the time I bought what I thought would be great soup. It wasn't inexpensive, but it was terrible! I remember thinking, *Will I ever learn?* And then there was the time that Marcus just had to try this new cereal. I want you to know that the voice inside my head told me to stick to my guns and tell him no. But you know how it is, he whined just a little too long and I was already tired and I thought, *It's only cereal. He'll eat it.* Guess what? Two bowls later, he announced, "I don't like that anymore!" How many times have I heard that? Well, I'm finished with my indecisive child, and I'm finished being a consumer sheep!

Sure, I've tried it all before. Make a list, stick to the list, don't go shopping hungry and stick to the outer aisles because that's where the fruits, veggies and dairy are located. This time, I'm going to try something completely new! I'm going to use what I have on hand, and I'm going to look upon the grocery store in a whole new light.

The grocery store is for many, a place of refuge. The grocery store can be the place where we can seal our celebration or ease our pain! And don't get me wrong, food is rightly tied to joyous occasions. Last year we gave our youngest son a choice for his birthday dinner. He chose king crab legs.

The weekends were always reserved for a big family breakfast including pancakes, bacon, French toast and omelets. Sunday dinner is an all-afternoon affair, no matter what is on the menu! I've given up trying to replicate my mother's homemade biscuits, partly because she claims that she can't remember how to make them anymore. I do have handwritten notes of several of her other great recipes, (those she could remember), tucked in my favorite cookbook! My parents are from the South, where most families had their own chickens and gardens and knew what it meant to use what you have.

So, instead of tossing out another pack of uneaten deli meat, I've (hopefully) broken a bad habit and, in the process, saved myself some time and money. I still love the grocery store, but now it's a healthy relationship!

Here We Go Again

———— ∿ ————

I am still working on my relationship with clutter.

"You haven't looked at it in seven years, so don't go through it now." That was Yvonne, helping me to truly clean out my unfinished basement for only the second time in the 14 years we lived there. This time, we'd bought a new house and were moving out.

The first time was ten years earlier when Patrick and I spent five hours one Saturday afternoon going through boxes, books, photo albums and Christmas decorations to weed it all out. That time I saw *Jurassic Park*-sized crickets and had to tell our boys we'd be finished soon, each time they opened the basement door and implored us to come upstairs because they were too scared to come downstairs.

We never finished the basement in that house, which made it a perfect storage area and dumping ground. The longer it went unfinished the more daunting the task became, until a neighbor gave us carpet one year. That gesture set the wheels in motion. Patrick said, "We're cleaning out this basement this weekend." I waivered. "What about the *Great Forest Park Balloon Race* or the den meeting or the opening of that new mall?" He gave me a blank stare. "We can get it all done." I didn't really believe him, but I knew we needed to clean.

That first cleaning allowed us to create areas of storage. There was the holiday section. Over there, you could find the furniture mart and around there, you'd see our music department complete with an old turntable and dozens of vinyl records. There were old track medals from high school, toys and photo albums filled with old, sticky pictures. *Was I ever that skinny? Was my hair ever that long? And whatever happened to that boyfriend?* I heard Patrick laugh and talk about how young he once looked. I threw out most of my college textbooks, but throwing away greeting cards was the most difficult thing for me. I still had cards I'd received when I left Cape Girardeau and wedding cards. And those cards with loving words that I'd gotten from Patrick when I was his girlfriend, before I become his wife.

With the second major basement cleaning, Yvonne and Sherry didn't care about saving things we didn't and weren't going to use. They were on a mission to get the items out and away. It was a bit embarrassing. I'd never had a bunch of friends come and help me do anything. I just felt unprepared and disorganized, and like I was putting too much work on them, because there was so much stuff everywhere!"

Yvonne filled big garbage bags, tossed them over her shoulder and trudged up and down the stairs, yelling at me to stop looking through stuff and simply get rid of it. My girlfriends told me, "If you were a military wife, you'd have this stuff packed and unpacked in short order." My response was, "Well, I'm not a military wife." I felt like I was in the middle of an intervention all afternoon except no one sat me down and said, "We love you but you have to get help for your packrat ways. There's a van waiting outside to take you to a clinic for women who can't throw anything away. Get in the van now. Get on the plane now. Go get the help you need or this relationship is over."

Thankfully, the fun overpowered all of that. But I'll admit, accepting that help wasn't easy.

I'm Not Into Cars

Are experiences that actually turn out to be lessons ever easy? Of course not! Not one! My Honda Pilot sitting in my garage has 165,000 miles on it and is the first car I ever paid off. I am so proud of that. I wanted to be the person who, when you asked how many miles I had on my car, could say, "Oh, 200,000 miles." I wanted to be that person. But, no.

For two years, Patrick had been saying, "You've got to start looking for a new car. Soon, this one will need repairs and have bigger expenses." I just didn't want another car note. Even when we found ourselves paying two mortgages he kept saying it, "You need another car. You need another car." I kept thinking, *No I don't! We need to sell that house!* I could not see two mortgages and a new car. I just couldn't see it. But he kept saying, "We can handle it. We're going to sell the house. We can handle it." He even said, "Let's go look at a car. I made an appointment and we're going to test-drive a car."

Let me admit that I have an unreasonable fear about the car-buying process. I have a lack of trust in myself and in car salesmen. I'm nervous about all the debt. I'm worried they'll take advantage. Fear: Unreasonable. Two mortgages: Unsustainable. New car: Out of the question!

Carol A. Daniel

All the while I'm thinking he should be happy that I'm not trying to take on new debt. I had been focused on saving. I was staying out of the mall and had cut back on the shoes. So, I was saving. But still, he was pushing like he knew something I didn't know.

So, we went to the dealer. I didn't even want to get out of the car. I don't know what I was so scared of. But he said, "These people are expecting us." I didn't care. I could tell he was upset. I said, "You go test-drive the car and let me know." So, he gets out and I stay in the car. I could feel his frustration. It was palpable. Then, he came back to the car to get his insurance card, but he couldn't find it. *What? Was I smiling?* Needless to say, he was even more frustrated. We never did test-drive that car.

Much, much later, he told me he was partly upset because he felt like I was acting as if he didn't know what he was talking about or what he was doing. You know – lack of respect. And you know, that was true, true, true. I was more caught up in my own fear.

On the way home, he said, "That's it, you find the car you want, and we'll get it." I didn't say anything, but I was thinking, *How am I going to do that? I don't know how to find a car. You know how to do that. You're 'Mr. Consumer Reports.'* That was wrong, just wrong. So, I didn't do anything. For weeks, for months, I didn't do anything. And I thought, *Fine, because I didn't want to get a car in the first place! Is he the only man in America with a wife who doesn't want a new car?*

98

I did nothing, but the car, my Honda, started doing something. Jerking and dropping out of gear while I was driving. So, when it was time for the 165,000-mile checkup, I told the technician to call my husband when he figured out what was wrong with it. Patrick had said that morning, "If the repair bill is more than a couple thousand dollars, we're not going to repair it – it doesn't make any sense." They called him around 1 pm and told him, "Your Honda needs a new transmission. That'll be $6,000!" Guess what? I had to get a new car. And the value of the old car had crashed.

Then I had all these mixed emotions. I didn't listen. I should have listened. Why did I let fear stop me from listening? Now what was I going to do? I suggested a second opinion. I thought it was the right thing to do. But we had no time. I needed a car immediately.

I was on every car website looking for my dream car, a red Mercedes SL-500. That was my dream. When I turned 50, I would have that car. So, Patrick said, "Try to find it and we'll test-drive it." This was all more tragic than it was funny...I found several. And we test-drove one that was the right year but it wasn't red. It was cabernet. We test-drove it and I was beside myself.

My 12-year-old, however, didn't want me to get a two-seater at all, saying, "Where are all of us going to fit?" I didn't care that it was a two-seater. Two people. The only time we all ride together is when we're going to church and PJ the teenager is not getting ready to ride with me too much anymore.

We got there and took the car out for a test drive. It was loud. It shook and made unidentified noises even though it was a car from one of the best dealerships in town. We took it on Highway 270 and when we got it up to a little speed, it started shaking like a bucket of bolts. I was devastated. It wasn't red anyway and it had an oil leak. The salesman said, "I wouldn't worry about that." And I thought, *Are you crazy? This is 'Mr. Consumer Reports,' who had been a mechanic in the Army!*

We walked away from that. Then I started listening. We test-drove six cars in two weeks, one of which we had to get out of because the previous owners had a dog and the smell was horrible. How did they not detail that car? It smelled like smoke and dog. We had to get out of the car after I started coughing and Patrick started sneezing.

Three of the cars were the brand he had recommended a year earlier, which at the time, I didn't even remember. I think Marcus reminded me that it was the kind Daddy had shown me. And that is what we eventually bought, the one he recommended, and I love it. I told him that I love it, and he looked at me sideways and said, "I knew that you would. I always thought you would look good in that car." Thank God for growth. He could have rubbed my nose in it and been very upset about the whole scenario.

We have to learn how to listen without fear. Being responsible is one thing, but don't cloak it in fear. Recognize when fear is driving your decisions.

A Will Unsigned

As of today, Patrick and I have a living will sitting in our attorney's office. However, it's unsigned.

When we first met with the attorney, we did so with the understanding that one of us may die first. We didn't even consider the possibility that both of us could die during the same horrible, tragic circumstance. "Who would care for the children then?" the attorney asked. Sitting at the long conference table, tears unexpectedly filling my eyes. I thought of my parents who are still alive. I wondered if they ever experienced this moment.

It's so terrible to consider but necessary to think about. Who would be best suited to raise our sons through the trauma of losing both parents? All three of my brothers are retired military officers, and my sister is a college admissions counselor. Patrick's youngest brother lives in St. Croix. He has two sisters, one of which has her hands full with three daughters in Atlanta.

I thought of my brother Al and his wife Stephanie. We live ten minutes apart and even attend the same church. I call her, "Mother Earth." She is a teacher and she makes the best yellow cake with chocolate

icing, from scratch. Once she even made care pack-
ages for not only their daughter Ashley, but for all of
Ashley's suite mates at the University of Illinois.
Since Ashley and her brother AJ are grown and
gone, Al and Stephanie are now empty nesters.
Would they want to take on two boys?

Patrick thought of his sister Martha and her husband Greg. When we met with the attorney, they
had no plans to have children. Since they didn't
have plans to have kids of their own, I was uncomfortable asking them to raise mine. They enjoyed
their freedom and traveled a lot. I wasn't sure they
would want to suddenly be tied down with two
boys. They now have an adorable son, but they live
in San Antonio. Would I want our boys to have to
leave their hometown, their school, friends and
church?

All of our siblings, I'm sure, would do a wonderful
job with our sons. I should feel great about having
such excellent choices.

My mother doesn't have a will. I've told her, "I don't
want to think about you dying, but I just don't want
you to leave us and leave so many unresolved issues
behind." She, like many, doesn't want to think about
the end, but she also doesn't want us to struggle
with her estate. Let me stop there and say that she
doesn't even think she has an estate in the first
place, but I know better. I've had to tell her over
and over again that just because we talk wills, health

directives, caskets and eulogies, doesn't mean she's dying tomorrow!

Patrick and I need to sign our will. And my mother needs to sign hers also.

Two Mortgages

"We have an offer coming in!"

Sweet words to my ears, but I knew better than to pop open a bottle of champagne just yet.

We'd been paying two mortgages for 13 months with no end in sight. Each time our realtor suggested a price drop, my husband would say, "I'm not just going to give my house away." But I was focused on the fact that not only had no one made an offer since it went on the market the year before, most of the reactions by those who saw it were eerily similar: "The busy road in the back is a deal breaker." I knew we couldn't move the road, and I knew we couldn't move the house, so I WAS nearly ready to give it away.

We began looking for a larger, nicer home about five years earlier. Though I liked much of what I saw, my husband pointed out numerous deficiencies or questionable design decisions that I never noticed. I remember telling him at one point, "You should go looking by yourself and then when you find something you like, take me to see it." He says I did the same thing when we looked for our first house. With an infant in tow and a new job in a new city, I got tired of looking pretty quickly, and he says that I told him, "Let's just buy this one, it's fine." And here we were again.

I was growing weary of all the looking, but he was on a perpetual scouting mission, refusing to give up until he found the right point guard for his team. Then our realtor stumbled across a row of houses tucked away in an area of town I knew nothing about. She called me that night, and we went out the next day. We walked in the door and cue the heavenly chorus. *Finally, a home we both loved!* Now we just needed to sell our house.

Mind you, the recession was going full steam at the time. But we were prepared for a jumbo mortgage. A part of my husband's DNA as a perpetual scout is to save money. So against my DNA, we had built something I never ever thought I'd have, a nest egg.

We moved forward with buying the house and then working to put ours on the market. The days began to darken in my heart. First of all, I know there are those who will pack your belongings for you and transport them to a different location in vehicles they have for that specific purpose. I think they are called movers. But my perpetual scout is a man's man, and he decided we could move ourselves, or as I call it, our family of four and our 16 years of marriage stuff. And so he did with a little help from his friends and very little help from me. The big bruise I saw on his arm the next day, coupled with his limp, confirmed for me that somehow, I had to stand my ground and hire the movers if we decided to put ourselves through this trauma again.

There is only one thing I hate more than packing and that is, you guessed it, unpacking. But I learned to hate something even more. Our realtor would send emails to us with comments from those who had walked through our house to see if it was worthy of their standards and their mortgage. The observations focused on different things, but the end result was nearly always the same.

"Backyard is wonderful." "Busy road is too loud." "Kitchen is great, but with small children, busy road is a concern." "Home shows well, buyers feel road out back is a deal breaker." And so it went.

It quickly became clear that the house was not going to fly off the market. I was a little more than disappointed. I was shell-shocked. How would we afford two mortgages? My husband kept the faith, but I began a juggling act with worry, resentment and hope. Here we were in our dream home, on a lake no less, but the dream was tainted by this ever-present reality of an empty, unsold house in the midst of the worst recession since the Depression. What would we do? When I was able to muster hope just in time for Patrick's occasional worry, I would ask him, "Do you feel that God had blessed us with our new home?"

He would answer, "Yes, I do." And with that, I explained that we had to believe that the other house would sell eventually.

Over the months, I couldn't help but reflect on those unlike us who had lost their homes to foreclosure, or who had lost their jobs and then their homes. Each time I saw a moving van on the highway or a car stuffed with boxes, clothing, hampers and stuffed animals, I wondered if it was someone who'd lost their home and had to move. And here I had people constantly asking me, "Do you love your new home?" I always hesitated because I couldn't answer the question. So much of my attention and emotion was on the house not selling. I could barely enjoy our new home. I had to keep reminding myself that we had prepared for this possibility and that we were miraculously able to pay the two mortgages. It is a place I still wouldn't wish on anyone. The stress is real, and my reaction to it was unreal. I thought I was more emotionally mature and spiritually steady than that. But I wasn't. What have I learned? I learned many things about my husband, our marriage, as well as real estate and myself. But central to the lesson of the year of two mortgages is to first HIRE MOVERS!

All I Ever Wanted

At first, *all I ever wanted* was to be a mother and a wife. Now all I want is for my children to truly believe in themselves and to be confident about their abilities. I want them to be educated, to be kind and compassionate. I want them to be leaders, first in their own lives, and I want them to be the kind of men that people know they can count on. I do want something for them that I cannot control...I want a world for them that doesn't look at them sideways or suspiciously. I want a world for them that doesn't discount them. I want a world for them in which they are not invisible.

PJ wants to invent – any inventor changes the world. And that's what I expect for him to do – to change the world. Since Marcus was five, he has wanted to be in the military (and a chef). Marcus wants to change the world. We have spent a great deal of time telling them that their lives are not even about them. Our marriage is not even about us, it's about them, to prepare them to be who they are to be for the rest of the world. That is legacy. I do want them to live outward, and we are trying to cultivate that sense of service in them. We have seen flashes of them in action already when they have spoken out and when they've seen someone in need without lunch money or being bullied. Even when they were little, holding doors and picking up things for people who'd dropped them. They've stepped up. Years ago I started praying for them, that they would know their purpose in life...because when they leave this house, and they know their purpose in life, then we've done a magnificent job.

One of the most difficult things with kids today is selfishness and a sense of entitlement. And that's our fault because some of us are that way too. They have so many gadgets, so many channels and so much to focus on, that they've come by it honestly.

But I want them to think, "Who am I to walk around selfish and entitled when there is so much need and so much work to be done?" Do PJ and Marcus know how rare they are with two parents married, successful and educated? They are bright, charming and handsome. They will go to college. And they have to give. Period. They have to. Who else is going to do it? God blessed them for a reason. When I think about it, God blessed me with them for a reason.

all i ever wanted

On the Beach in Florida
Marcus, PJ and Patrick

My Deep Voice

Some lessons take much longer to unfold than others. Growing up with such a deep voice that many mistook me for a boy was a long, long lesson.

"Son, can I talk to your mother?" I dealt with that question countless times when, growing up, I would dare to answer the phone.

When I was a junior at Lincoln University, a fellow student (a guy) once said, "You need to take some of that bass out of your voice." Each of those comments left me feeling a little less than feminine, a little less than confident in the most basic self-expression tool we have, our voice.

But my, how perceptions, attitudes and careers can change. If all those folks who felt I sounded like a boy or sounded too masculine could have been with me this morning (or on any given day in my broadcast career), they would not know what to think. For that matter, neither do I. You see, I grew up hating my voice. I saw it as a hindrance and later as a reason certain boys, and men, did not find me attractive. But, I couldn't change it. It's what God gave me. So what's a girl to do? Use what God gave you, that's what.

When I decided to major in broadcasting, I still didn't

think I had a good voice. I thought it was flat and unattractive until one news director took the time to listen and give me a written critique. He told me that it was good, something he had never heard before. He also told me to be more natural in my delivery and to try not to sound like I was reading or reciting information. Then he told me that he felt good, solid female voices are hard to find and that I should stick with it.

Whew! No more, "Son, can I talk to your mother," for me. I was ready to take on the world. Or was I?

That one good review certainly lifted my self-image, but it didn't change it completely. Secretly, I still felt like my voice was odd. I couldn't imagine making a living or that people would want to hear me, but something propelled me forward. Little by little, year after year, I stopped thinking about when I was the nine-year-old girl whose dentist thought she sounded like a boy. I started listening to the compliments and being amazed and thankful for them.

I was sitting in a production studio in St. Louis, reading a script for a couple of videos, when a thought hit me. *Here I am using the voice that I once had such disdain for.* Even more amazing to me is the fact that as a radio personality, most people don't know what I look like, and yet they can identify me by my voice.

And more amazing still is there are times when I answer the phone at work and someone on the other end will say, "Sir, can I talk to your news director?"

My response is, "Sure. Can you hold on while I get him for you?"

That insecure little girl with the booming voice has turned into a professional broadcaster and a woman who knows who she is and what she has to offer.

A NOTE FROM THE PUBLISHER
Mission Possible Press...
Creating Legacies through Absolute Good Works

As a publisher, I have the opportunity to transform hopeful writers into successful authors. This brings me great pleasure because I believe everyone has wisdom to share and valuable stories to tell.

Prior to publication, I worked with Carol to help her choose which aspects of her big heart and busy life she would share. Listening to and capturing her stories was an experience in itself! Carol is doing so much and she's busy, tired and at times overwhelmed because she cares so much. She truly wants to be there for everyone and do everything–something that is not nearly possible. I admire her willingness to share her life, her struggles and her time because she is such a bright light in this sometimes-gloomy world.

They say time flies when you're having fun—and it's always a pleasure to be in Carol's presence. What this woman has done in her 30 years in media has been remarkable and wonderful for the St. Louis Metropolitan Region. What she has yet to do for the world is spine tingling. With talent, beauty, grace, strong opinions and a true sense of self and family, Carol Daniel is a force to be admired, embraced and reckoned with.

When I saw Carol at The Best Steak House that winter night, I knew she needed to get some things off her shoulders and just believed that I was mighty enough to help take some of the load. Her husband, Patrick, observed and encouraged – something, I've learned, he does very well!

So many struggle to find their voice, life purpose and place in today's world. What Carol shares is a unique voice that can be heard, trusted and embraced.

Thanks to Carol, we are continuing to make the *Mission Possible—creating legacies, inspiring, and building up—especially for women.* I am honored and pleased to present this book as part of our Extraordinary Living Series.

In the Spirit of Communication,
Jo Lena Johnson,
Founder and Publisher

Mission Possible Press, a division of Absolute Good
MissionPossiblePress.com

About the Author

Carol Daniel is first and foremost a mother and wife. She is also a 30-year veteran of broadcasting, eventually earning the title of *Triple Threat in the Media*. She is an award-winning columnist, writing about motherhood, marriage and politics. She was also the original co-host of an Emmy-winning lifestyle television show for women in St. Louis. She remains a news anchor for one of the leading news talk radio stations in the country. She has interviewed a wide variety of people from President Jimmy Carter and O.J. Simpson to then-U.S. Senate candidate Barack Obama. Carol is a gifted motivational speaker who loves nothing more than making her audiences laugh, and think, and then, go and conquer! She has always been proud to call herself a "military brat." Carol lives in the St. Louis area with her husband and two sons.

CPSIA information can be obtained at www.ICGtesting.com
Printed in the USA
LVOW010422230213

321248LV00003B/8/P

9 780985 276041